KEEP IT SIMPLE

Fiction

The Sterile Cuckoo
The Wizard of Loneliness
The Milagro Beanfield War
The Magic Journey
The Nirvana Blues
A Ghost in the Music
American Blood
An Elegy for September

Nonfiction

If Mountains Die (with William Davis)
The Last Beautiful Days of Autumn
On the Mesa
A Fragile Beauty
The Sky's the Limit

KEEP IT SIMPLE

A DEFENSE OF THE EARTH

TEXT AND PHOTOGRAPHS BY

JOHN NICHOLS

W · W · NORTON & COMPANY · NEW YORK · LONDON

The text of this book is composed in Bodoni Book,
with the display set in Antique Roman.
Composition by Zimmering, Zinn & Madison, Inc.
Manufacturing by Dai Nippon Printing Co., Ltd., Tokyo, Japan.

Library of Congress Cataloging-in-Publication Data

Nichols, John.
    Keep it simple: a defense of the earth/text and photographs by
John Nichols.
        p.   cm.
    1. Landscape photography.   I. Title.
TR660.5.N494   1992
779'.36—dc20   91–40415

ISBN 0-393-03386-4
ISBN 0-393-30901-0 (pbk)

W.W. Norton & Company, Inc., 500 Fifth Avenue, New York, N.Y. 10110
W.W. Norton & Company Ltd., 10 Coptic Street, London WC1A 1PU

1 2 3 4 5 6 7 8 9 0

To my good friend and
cohort in crime—

Bill Rusin

In loving memory of
Santa Fe Adobe Style,
Las Vegas Neon, and
Autumn in Maine.

RIP

KEEP IT SIMPLE

We all know the way it works, which is as follows:

You have a successful career; you're rich and famous and adored by millions. You're married to the most glamorous, sensitive, intelligent, understanding, exciting person on earth. When you fly to Paris, you always take the Concorde and stay at the Hôtel de Senlis on the rue Malbranche. Your children are compassionate; they get straight As in school; they win blue ribbons at the Science Fair. And they'd never think of ingesting crack, smack, pot, or PCP. You've done the "Today" show six times, Johnny Carson an even dozen, David Letterman twice. Your latest book/movie/compact disc or choreography job has been hailed as a masterpiece, and naturally it went platinum, was a best seller, won a Tony. *People* magazine declares you one of the twenty-five most fascinating individuals on earth. And Robert Redford is either directing, or starring in, the story of your life.

Then everything goes to hell in a hand basket.

For starters, you're overextended: eleven meetings a day, a speech every night, endless travel. It becomes harder and harder to spend quality time with the kids. To keep alert on the concert stage, or during the penning of Chapter Thirty-Six of your next blockbuster, you pop a few uppers one day, half a dozen the next morning, a whole bottle the third afternoon. You also discover it's easier to unwind at the end of a long session with a double shot of Stoly on the rocks, no twist. Make that a couple of doubles with a Dos XX chaser.

Pretty soon you start feeling lonely, because you're always in New York while your spouse is in L.A. And lo and behold, suddenly that cute little guy/babe on a barstool near the jukebox looks pretty good. Tammy Wynette is crooning "Stand by Your Man," the lighting is low, and one come-hither glance leads to another. . . .

Next thing you know, it's front-page dirt in the tabloids. FAMOUS AESTHETE CAUGHT DANCING NAKED IN DUPONT CIRCLE FOUNTAIN

WITH TRANSVESTITE CHICKEN HAWK! Your spouse goes crazy and demands a divorce. Your eldest kid is busted for imbibing illicit chemicals in the backseat of a pink Lamborghini belonging to a noted child pornographer. Abruptly, you realize that a double sawbuck (squared) in toot is disappearing up your own beak on a daily basis. You have to cancel a couple of dates. The impresarios sue...and win. Your editor says the latest novel ain't worth the paper they won't print it on. Your better half tries to commit suicide...in front of Grauman's Chinese Theater...with seventeen paparazzi in attendance.

Naturally, you promptly OD on phenobarbitals, and they rush you, comatose, to the hospital. Fortunately Dr. Kildare saves your dismal life, but upon release there's no place to go to except a homeless shelter, where you "live" for about six months in a stupor created by a California Tokay that sells for $1.69 a keg.

Miraculously, the day before you're slated to die, a lightning bolt slams out of the sky and whacks you in the noggin. "Eureka!" you cry. "I've found Jesus!" And overnight you clean up the act. Goodbye, codependency trips; hello, Betty Ford rehab nabobs! It's six weeks of pure hell, but you survive, turn vegetarian, and emerge a new person. Your next book/CD/movie is a smash hit. "I'm drug-free and proud of it," you chortle on a national television PSA. There's a new honey in your life even cuter (and younger) than the last one, and all the children are back to their precollapse 4.0 scholastic averages. *People* magazine does an eight-page spread on how you fell to the depths, found God, got straight, hit the commercial jackpot again, and plan to live happily ever after. The new babe/toy boy on your arm grins like a Cheshire cat.

And all's well that ends well—qué no?

Fair enough. And although I'm not here to burden you with all the lurid details, I myself recently went through something like the above-mentioned scenario, and to date I have survived to tell the tale.

Granted, I am neither rich nor particularly famous, and I never had a drug, or much of an alcohol, problem. In general, my children seem no more insane than your average North American skinhead jive rap slamdancers. And not for all the money in China would I ever, even in my wildest dreams, set foot in a supersonic Concorde.

And as for Jesus? Basically I'm a Marxist who believes religions are the opiates of the masses. Plus there is nothing on either of my arms right now except a secondhand sweater I bought two years back for $1.98.

Nevertheless, not all that long ago I, too, had a life so professionally complicated, emotionally chaotic, logistically absurd, and spiritually fractured that I didn't know which end was up. And naturally, as often happens in these cases, I soon hit a brick wall going ninety and wound up in a hospital with a pain in my chest and a telemetry monitor in the breast pocket of my hospital-issue PJs.

I advised my agent to get in touch with *People*. He got on the horn immediately, but they weren't interested: "John *who*?"

Meanwhile, doctors put me through a battery of tests— echograms, Dopplers, thalium treadmills. They concluded that perhaps I had already suffered a cardiac attack. It was decided to catheterize my heart, shoot it full of dye, and check out the arteries. So down to the basement I went, modern technology performed its miracle, and the doctors announced, "Nope, the arteries look great."

Then they put me on digitalis for the rest of my life.

Well, as soon as I arrived back home, what was left of my brain started thinking. I was forty-eight years old and mighty tired. I had been a very lucky person in my life, and I certainly wanted to live for another fifty years. But the way I felt inside, I was looking at maybe another fifty days, max. If the warm weather held and the digitalis kicked in real quick.

So I thought to myself: *John, I think it's time for a change*.

"What kind of change?" I replied hesitantly, defensive and worried.

Well, I'm a physical person. When in doubt, I like to move the parts of my body and feel wind in my hair. It's one way I have of calming down. So I trundled outside, located my rusty old bike, and tugged it clear of the weeds. I gave it a quick lube and adjusted a few things, then mounted up and began to pedal. Not very fast, mind you. In fact, I merely dawdled along, and pretty soon the lazy motion created in me a rather pleasant torpor.

And as I drifted south, I made the first important decision related to the creation of a new me.

To wit:

"From now on, you're riding this bike."

A few minutes later I parked my conveyance in a chicory tangle beside a barbed-wire fence and entered a field of blossoming thistles, many of them higher than my head. Bumblebees busily trenchered among the bristles, gathering pollen. And I remained quite still for a very long spell, captivated by their gentle uproar.

In the blue sky overhead a couple of clouds were dawdling. And an interesting event took place: I relaxed. And I could actually feel it happen. Something drained out of my body, leaving behind not only exhaustion but also a downright exotic sense of relief. And a question occurred to me: *Why am I killing myself?* And an answer came back: *It's okay, you don't have to kill yourself anymore, it's not all that important anyway. Reject the chaos for a while, kick back and mellow out, learn to see things in a different light, find a way to keep it all more simple*.

Simple.

That seemed to be the key. Suddenly, I had an almost desperate yearning for *simplicity*.

That very night I sat down to browse through Henry David Thoreau. I'd read him before—often. I had used quotations from his work to make many points—in my own speeches, articles, and books. On this particular evening I opened directly to page 74 in my Rinehart *Walden*, and found myself confronting this exhortation:

Our life is frittered away by detail. An honest man has hardly need to count more than his ten fingers, or in extreme cases he may add his ten toes, and lump the rest. Simplicity, simplicity, simplicity! I say, let your affairs be as two or three, and not a hundred or a thousand: instead of a million count half a dozen, and keep your accounts on your thumb-nail.

On the following page, his diatribe continued:

Simplify, simplify. Instead of three meals a day, if it be necessary eat but one; instead of a hundred dishes, five; and reduce other things in proportion.

And on page 76 he added:

Why should we live with such hurry and waste of life? We are determined to be starved before we are hungry. Men say that a stitch in time saves nine, and so they take a thousand stitches today to save nine to-morrow. As for *work*, we haven't any of any consequence. We have the Saint Vitus' dance, and cannot possibly keep our hands still.

I closed the book and reminded myself: "This guy wrote that stuff a hundred and thirty-five years ago." I had read it for the first time in 1957. And now, thirty-two years after that, *finally* it makes an indelible impression. So why didn't I heed his message the first time around and plan my life accordingly?

I spent a long while that night just thinking about things. Life on earth in general . . . and my own existence specifically. Eventually I reached my own conclusion that it was time to begin again from scratch. I did not have a clear idea of how to accomplish this, but felt sure I knew what *didn't* work. And even that can be a starting point.

By the time I fell asleep, I had begun to form a plan. And apropos my spontaneous decision of that afternoon, I decided my first revolutionary act would be a real commitment to my bicycle. That'd slow me down, but good, and then—who knows?—perhaps a more reasonable life would follow.

Understand, we are not talking here about a hi-tech six-hundred-dollar yuppie Rockhopper mountain bicycle with megatread off-road tires and twenty-eight gears. No, my prosaic piece of machinery, a monument to the recycling ethic, was real rudimentary. I had located the frame in a dump, the rear tire in a junkshop; the front tire was salvaged from a ditch. A little oil, a few screws, and some TLC had made it all come together semicoherently. The vehicle had three forward speeds, but mostly I used only a single gear—the one in the middle. And although the gearing system was a prehistoric Sturmey-Archer rig invented around 1100 B.C., it worked just fine.

At the outset I determined never to ride my bike swiftly, nor would I endulge in wheelies or other invigorating acrobatics—too dangerous. I would simply plod along at a speed slightly more vertiginous than the mph achieved by old conestogas heading west, and that way I could see—and *enjoy*—where I was going. And of course I would never fume during the delays of traffic jams, I'd simply glide right through them.

If something went wrong with my bike, the essentially moronic tools I carried in my knapsack could rectify the situation. I'm referring to a tiny patch kit ($1.89), three tube removal tools ($2.98), and a small crescent wrench ($2.29). At home I kept a tin of Sturmey-

Archer cycle oil ($3.50). If I added but six drops of goo to my rear axle once a month, the can would last a lifetime. I also bought a tube of Bullshot bearing grease ($2.75), which might run out in eight to eleven years.

And that would be the maintenance costs of my machine.

What interested me most about my bicycle, however, was the role it could play as metaphor. Starting with its simplicity. And the lack of damage it did—to everything. Truth is, I felt downright self-righteous on the day I abandoned my Dodge D150 slant-six pickup truck and converted to self-locomotion.

Meet St. John of the Velocipede, with two shiny halos for his wheels!

Of course, for a while, on the bike, it took much longer to complete my chores every day. Then I simply eliminated half the chores. And today, two years later, I've reached a point where I can accomplish but a third of what I once did, in twice the time it used to take. But I commit only a fraction as much environmental damage en route. And, incredibly, my blood pressure is down, my heart is stronger, my health is better in every way. Too, I've learned that much of what I thought I had to achieve was irrelevant and unnecessary.

And furthermore, most of it was stupid.

So: *Je pense, donc je suis.*

Then I wed myself to the bicycle.

And everything else was up for grabs.

Basically, I stopped the world and got off. I retreated to a small (hidden) two-room apartment and inaugurated a very low profile. I ordered a new unlisted phone number and left the machine unplugged most of the day (and night). It was nearly impossible for the outside world to get in touch. And anyway, I wasn't in much of a talking mood. I had lost a five-year marriage and the house I'd occupied for twenty years. Into the bargain, I was almost broke. It was time to hunker down . . . lick my wounds . . . and heal.

I began therapy by taking a lot of time off. For days I wandered in the mountains near home, toting a knapsack full of guidebooks to the birds, flowers, mushrooms. I started eating leisurely breakfasts in my favorite café while luxuriating in the newspapers or merely chatting with friends. I even put new strings on my old guitar and played music for the first time in a decade.

Though I've always considered myself a novelist at heart, during my former helter-skelter life I'd had no time for reading fiction. So now I made it a point always to have a novel going. And to open it every day. And I began to savor writing again with a fervor akin to the one generated in me by literature way back during college days.

My former life had been dominated by obligations—to speak, to organize, to attend meetings, to write articles, to read manuscripts, to answer letters, to say yes. Now, gradually, I learned to say no—politely . . . and often. And on those occasions when it became necessary either to default or to let things slide, I actually refused to wallow in guilt. My *Übermensch* days were over.

I needed to catch up on sleep—*years* of sleep. So when I grew tired at night, instead of pushing to exhaustion, as had been my wont, I simply went to bed. I never scheduled an appointment before noon. And, even after waking, I often lay on my mattress, drowsing, for hours. I actually trained myself to rediscover the pleasures of being lazy. And I returned to my old habit of taking an afternoon siesta.

Eventually, the sense of urgency which had driven me so hard for so long drained out of my brain, then from my muscles, and finally clear of my bones.

And then one day I picked up a camera again.

For years I had recorded on film the valley in which I live. Most of the photographs were of wide open spaces, huge skies, magnificent weather. I was drawn to the grandeur of large-scale landscapes, which had properly reflected my mood at the time. In due course the pictures had become a sort of diary of my outlook on things. But when life became too hectic, I stopped wandering in wild country with a tripod over my shoulder.

Yet now, whenever I took out a camera, I had little desire to visit my former haunts. To a considerable degree, I had modified the boundaries of that previous world. For starters, on a bicycle my range was pretty limited. So instead of traipsing off to record another plethora of Wagnerian sunsets, I soon found myself focusing on more mundane objects closer to home. A dead wasp on my towel rack . . . a pink tulip in the miniature lawn . . . the shiny bell of my bicycle. And it wasn't long before I found myself pleasantly surprised by all the pictures I could make of seemingly routine subject matter. In an ordinary blossom, bone, or shadow resided a fascinating calm for me. And inevitably I concluded: There's no need to seek hyperbole in order to praise the earth.

As usual, the unassuming pictures I made during this time jibed perfectly with my mood. They joined the healing process, reflecting the goals I was striving to achieve. Anthill pebbles or lichens on a gravestone may seem like prosaic fare, yet by paying attention to these matter-of-fact wonders, I sure quieted my soul.

Later, as I began to feel better and ventured out into the larger world again, I carried along a new sense of proportion. It brought both the politics of my daily struggle and the rhythm of my personal adventure closer to a workable equilibrium.

And my photographs seemed like a record of that metamorphosis.

Now:

For a long time I had considered myself a political human being. It was always important that my life and work be guided by a social conscience and commitment. I suppose I thought of myself as a relatively unselfish person. And so at first I felt pretty uncomfortable, even indulgent, for spending time putting my own life back together. Yet not too far into the process I concluded that perhaps the first truly important political act *any* person of conscience makes ought to be extending a hand to themself. Maybe it's as simple as the old adage that charity begins at home. For sure, you can't save the world if you can't save yourself.

And if you're dead, you're useless.

Of course, you can't separate individual struggle from universal implications either. My well-being depends on the planet; the planet's health depends on me. "Whenever we try to pick out anything by itself," said the naturalist John Muir, "we find it hitched to everything else in the universe." So at the bottom of trying to fashion a simple (and healthy) existence is the necessity to protect the very web of life itself.

For years I had considered myself an "environmentalist." But when I stripped away the clutter and confronted my own personal habits, it seemed I still had a long way to go before achieving eco-sainthood. Not that I deliberately set out each morning to devastate the planet. But through an omission here, a careless gesture there, I was certainly doing my part to trash the future. Not to mention how I had already trashed myself.

So I quickly vowed to tread with a lighter step, which meant trying to mitigate even the smallest act with a deliberately benevolent intent.

I began to clean up the environment by changing my diet. I quit drinking coffee and soda pop, backed way off on the booze, and redoubled my efforts not to eat salt, sugars, and other similar poisons. I switched grocery stores, buying organic if possible—fruits, vegetables, pasta...hardly any meat. Though I had never been a person who scarfed tons of food, then joined a spa to work it off, I now redoubled my efforts to eat sensibly, in moderation. And I was amazed at how much better I could feel.

Then I tackled my relationship with a consumer society whose rapacious demands seem like a formula for planetary suicide. I tried harder than ever not to purchase things unless they were essential. Naturally, I recycled all bottles, cans, glass, newspapers. Instead of buying periodicals, I began to read them in the library. I avoided heavily packaged products. In the grocery store I never put my tomatoes, cucumbers, or avocados in plastic bags, and I carted home all comestibles in my knapsack. The apartment I rent has an electric hot-water heater, but I soon learned that if I flipped on the breaker switch only a half hour before taking a shower and turned it off immediately afterward, I could save sixty bucks a month on the electric bill.

And, yes, I even turned off the lights when not using them. And refused to accumulate gadgets: no hair dryers, no Water Piks, no Exercycles...no Weed Eaters. Instead of giving lavish gifts to the family at Christmas, I began sending donations to organizations fighting for the earth. I bought my clothes secondhand at a place in Albuquerque called Thriftown, where a hundred bucks every two years kept me in pants, shirts, sport coats, winter jackets, sneakers, belts—fashion seemed irrelevant. I quit buying manila envelopes, choosing instead to recycle what people sent to me or what I fished from trash cans at the post office. I also started writing almost all the first drafts of my books by hand on the backs of junk mail. Eventually, I transposed them to type by means of an old Olympia portable (nonelectric) machine that belongs in the Jurassic period of technology. And if I earned money beyond my needs, I tried to redistribute the wealth. Granted, long ago I had understood that whatever my income, living in a style as if I made five thousand dollars a year was a good way to maintain my independence, avoiding all the traps. But now I really cranked on towing that particular line.

Thoreau again:

Most of the luxuries and many of the so-called comforts of life, are not only not indispensable, but positive hinderance to the elevation of mankind.

My list could go on and on—but there's no need to beat a dead horse. And if I seem too good to be true in my newly achieved state of blissful simplicity, believe me, it's an illusion. My life still reeks of personal contradictions and self-destructive impulses, and probably always will. To boot, they continue chopping down trees and operating pulp mills to manufacture my books. And I hate to think of the chemicals used to print this volume, let alone the labor relations between the workers and management involved. Barring a weird "miracle," nobody will get rich off *Keep It Simple*, yet the profit motive makes it all possible, and *that* contradiction has me pretty uncomfortable.

Obviously, I have decided that the good of this tome offsets the bad, and getting the message out is worth it. At least I hope that's the case. After all, the earth is in a state similar to my own on the day I entered the hospital, and we can't push it much closer to the brink. There's no need here for me to give yet another of my traditional litanies about pollution, ozone holes, greenhouse effect, third world poverty, and human exploitation; daily newspaper and TV reports assure that most of us are now well informed on these matters. The only relevant question anymore is: What, if anything, are we going to do about it?

I hope the answer involves a worldwide commitment to the kind of life I felt compelled to forge in order to keep my own self ambulatory, quasi happy, and useful.

Naturally, I have a manifesto.

The collective existence we all should be gearing toward cannot be as complex or as noisy or as greedy and wasteful as the world that exists today, not by a long shot. Of necessity it must be simple, almost Spartan, I imagine . . . yet that should mean it will be much more beautiful. I think a "lowered" standard of living would actually remove a lot of pressure and angst from all our lives.

Says the poet Walter Lowenfels:

When the tragedy of the world market no longer dominates our existence, unexpected gradations of being in love with being here will emerge.

Certainly I have a vision of a human community more in balance with the rest of the planet and with its own myriad tribes and nations and nationalities. I picture an international economy based no longer on profit but on the needs of everyone concerned. I envision the renewable wealth of the planet—carefully developed to avoid waste—distributed evenly among all of us. And the energy we use to stay alive will come from the wind and sun and projects geothermal. All cultures will be honored, neither economic nor military imperialism will be tolerated, and we will have checked the population growth of our species in order to assure the survival of all species. I dream of cities without automobiles, a decentralized agriculture again, and a lack of mobility around the world offset by a wonderful stability that comes from *roots*, the true foundation of all good community and trust among peoples.

If cynics ridicule me for being an idealist, for fabricating utopias in the sky, I reply that it's only by making attempts at such a utopia that any future will exist at all.

And at least we need to dream.

In light of the current desperate world situation, people around me often throw up their hands and cry, "But what can I do?" My answer is almost always in this vein: Begin anywhere, but begin. Stop smoking, lay off the booze, ride a bicycle. Next, get rid of the air conditioner, junk the Winnebago, quit poisoning the lawn to keep it green. Then protest U.S. energy policies, third world exploitation, nuclear power plants. *Demand* simplicity.

And it might not hurt to browse through the pictures in this book. Per se they have no deep implications, no convoluted ax to grind. But they were a part of my therapy. And they are a visual record of my survival. And they ask for mercy.

I hope these photographs suggest a way of setting the mood for dealing with a planet up for grabs. Certainly they are my way of sharing with everyone how I stop to smell the flowers.

E. F. Schumacher wrote a book to prove that "Small is beautiful." Wendell Berry has rhapsodized about agricultural minds "that are programmed to Think Little." As he perished at the stake, the last words of a Czech hero and martyr, John Huss, were: "Oh holy simplicity!" According to Henry Miller, "The nature of the miraculous is—utter simplicity." And George Sand put it this way: "Simplicity is the essence of the great, the true, and the beautiful in art."

And also, of course, in life.

In that spirit these photographs are tendered: as gifts from my own personal struggle . . . and in hopes for a more compassionate future.

Tulip

Wild milkweed

Funny face

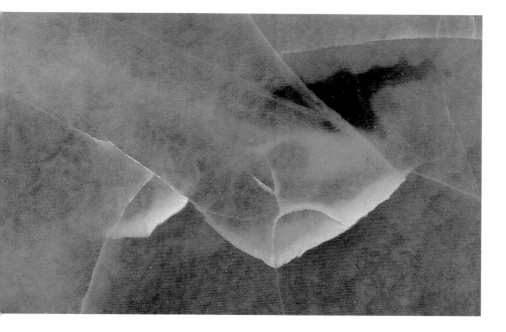

Cracked ice

Anthill

Grasses

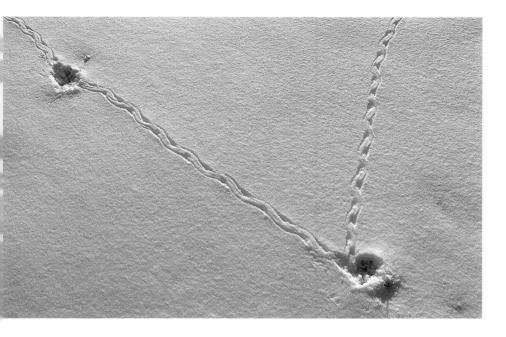

Horned lark feeding

Leaf

Bicycle bell

Rose petal

Old door

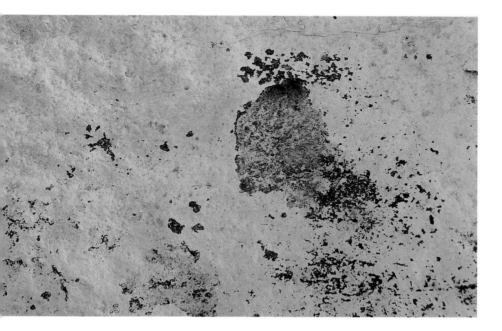

Igneous rock

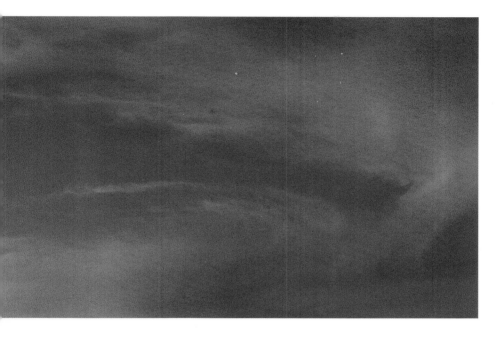

Pink cloud

Firm foundation

Night

Day

Jawbone

Brown trout

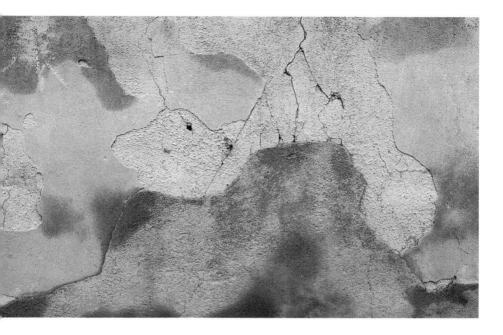

Old wall

Red flower

Tiny frog

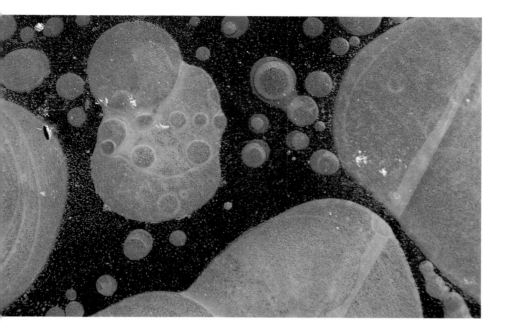

Air bubbles

Early morning

Eternity

Modern art

Abstract expressionism

Forsythia

Gravestone

Elm tree (day)

Elm tree (night)

Butterfly

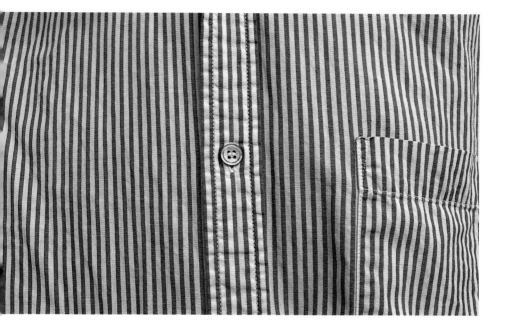

Button

Ladder

Window

Airplane

Towel rack

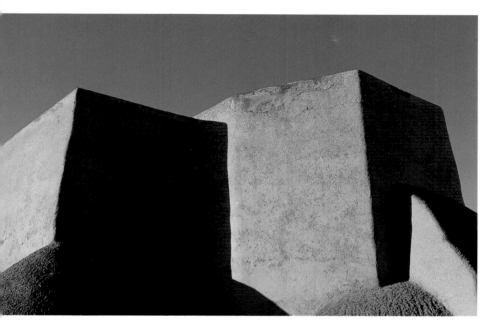

Church

Mirror

Piñon trees

Lilac blossoms

Foliage

Lack of foliage

Thin black wire

Thin white cloud

Yellow apple

Road to nowhere

Two splashes

Two horses

Two chairs

Two birds

Two stones

One ripple

Winter

Summer

Little bush

Big bush

Quiet puddle

Noisy puddle

Tres Orejas Mountain

Ute Mountain

Stock pond

Chevy Impala

Brake lights

Dangerous curve

Big city

Uncertain future

Human being (urban setting)

Human being (rural setting)

Reverence for life

Reverence for death

Choose life . . .

... it makes more sense